D1485974

INSPIRATIONS
'Recipes for Success'

with
Douglas and Lesley Mitch
at the Unicorn Inn Restaurant
Kincardine-on-Forth
Scotland

Mitch Publishing

Copyright © 1996
Douglas and Lesley Mitch
All Rights Reserved

Compiled by
Brian Cowan

Cover Photograph by
Jan Van der Merwe, Dollar.

Typesetting & Design by
Jane & Walter Sommerville, Balgownie Card Co., Culross.

Printed in Scotland by
Derek & Gill Nisbet, A4 Print, Dunfermline.

Bound by
J Shepherd & Son, Ltd., Edinburgh.

ISBN 0-9529340-0-0

Mitch Publishing
The Unicorn Inn Restaurant
Excise Street
Kincardine-on-Forth
Scotland

INTRODUCTION

Most of us have one. Some of us keep them to ourselves. Some of us share them with our family. Some of us talk about them at every opportunity. The one thing we nearly all have in common is that we do nothing about them!

Douglas and Lesley Mitch are slightly different - six years ago they gave up everything they had and took the first steps on a journey to make their '*dream*' come true.

At first sight The Unicorn Inn in Kincardine-on-Forth was certainly not the stuff that dreams are made of. It was a run-of-the-mill pub in a small village on the banks of the River Forth, known only for its proximity to the Kincardine Bridge. However, the village itself is steeped in history and is at the geographical crossroads of three counties. Douglas and Lesley saw a potential in the place that no-one else did - it was the perfect situation for their restaurant. Next stop was an appointment with their bank manager.

In 1990 they were living in a very comfortable converted farmhouse at the side of a golf course in Fife. They seemed to have everything including two beautiful daughters, Abby and Katy. Douglas had ten successful years in sales behind him and Lesley ran her own dried flower business from home. As a result, they had a lifestyle most people would envy.

When they announced they were giving all this up and risking everything they had to buy The Unicorn Inn to turn it into a Mediterranean style restaurant most people nodded and smiled politely. In private they laughed and even questioned their sanity, but, as is often said, "He who laughs last....!"

Douglas and Lesley are passionate about food and when, as a young couple, they spent some months travelling round Europe they became inspired by Mediterranean cuisine and over the next 10 years their idea marinated.

They always believed a successful restaurant did not just depend on good food but on friendly efficient service and the right ambiance.

Their vision was to create a restaurant which blended all of these qualities; a place where people could relax, have fun and enjoy fine food and wine from a constantly changing menu. They set about transforming the Unicorn with energy and determination. I think most people who have visited the restaurant would agree that their dream *has* come true.

The mythical unicorn was a one off, a unique animal. Douglas and Lesley are a unique couple and at the Unicorn Inn they have created a unique restaurant.

Partnership is the key to their success. They each have a defined role. Douglas's talent lies in creating the main menu, while Lesley's forté is sweets and puddings. When it comes to new ideas though, they inspire each other.

They live on the premises and have managed to combine family life with working life, not an easy feat with two young daughters to look after, but as Douglas says, "*Running the restaurant beats working for a living.*"

The restaurant has won numerous awards. It appears in the famous Michelin Restaurant Guide and has just been awarded 2 rosettes in the "AA Best Restaurants in Britain Guide" for the third consecutive year. Douglas and Lesley are currently resident chefs on 'Scotland Today', Scottish Television's lunchtime programme. One of the benefits of the television work is that it has forced Douglas to write down his recipes which, until now, have only been stored in his head. This in turn has created the opportunity for this book - a selection of recipes for dishes that have appeared on the Unicorn's menu over the past six years.

The Mitch's began cooking as enthusiastic amateurs. They are now self-taught, award-winning chefs. They realise how intimidating some recipe books can be and, in this book, they endeavour to keep things simple while still creating exciting "Unicorn" dishes. They want you to look at a recipe and say, *"I can do that"*.

As Douglas and Lesley would say - "*Enjoy!!!!*"

Brian Cowan

Look out for
Sebastian the Lobster.
He'll give you
some good advice!

For years, Friday nights were very special to us - we would open a bottle of wine and talk for hours about our dream, inspiring each other with ideas for our restaurant.

This inspiration eventually helped us turn our dream into reality.

We still search for inspiration every day - it may be in a book, on holiday or in each other.

We hope this book of 'Inspirations' will inspire you!!

Douglas & Lesley.

STARTERS

Moules Marinière
Roasted Red Pimientos with
a Black Olive Tapenade
Tiger Prawns in Garlic Butter
Warming Mediterranean Avocados
Seared Fresh Chicken Livers
Scottish Smoked Mackerel Mousse
Halloumi Cheese (Pan-fried with Capers)
Kimshi
Greek Village Salad
Pan-Fried Garlic Mushrooms
Smoked Salmon & Mussel Broth
Chilled Spanish Water Melon with Minted Oranges
Brian's Tomato & Red Pepper Soup
Portuguese Style Sardines
Steamed Haggis with a Drambuie, Cream & Grainy
Mustard Sauce

Moules Marinière

(serves 4)

This starter is within easy reach of everyone who can get their hands on good fresh mussels.

Deep rope mussels tend to be very consistent in quality and because they are grown on ropes suspended above the sea bed are completely "grit free".

INGREDIENTS:

3lb (1.4kg) Fresh Mussels
2 Glasses Dry White Wine
6 Shallots *(finely diced)*
1 Garlic Clove *(chopped)*
Sea Salt & Ground Black Pepper
Wedge of Lemon for Squeezing

Heat all the above ingredients, apart from the mussels, in a pot with a tight fitting lid.

Bring to the boil, remove the lid and allow to boil for 2-3 minutes.

Keep boiling vigorously, add the mussels and put the lid over the pot.

The mussels should open up when cooked (2-3 mins) - serve right away, discarding any shells that have not opened.

Be careful not to overcook them or they'll become rubbery!

 Clean the mussels thoroughly before cooking. "Debearding" means removing the stringy beard which can be found gathered on the mussel. Any mussels that are open and don't close when tapped sharply - discard.

Roasted Red Pimientos with a Black Olive Tapenade

(serves 4)

Peppers make a delightful starter and go particularly well with black olives. The Tapenade can be made in advance and stored in the fridge.

INGREDIENTS:
4 Large Red Peppers
2 Tablespoons Olive Oil

Rub the peppers with olive oil and line the base of a clean roasting tray with the remainder. Put into a medium oven (150°C / Gas Mark 2) and turn every five minutes. Cook until the peppers become blackened on the outside and slightly limp (approx. 25 mins). Remove from the oven and set aside until you can handle them without burning your fingers! With a sharp knife, peel off the outer skin and you should be left with a bright red pepper. Cut into quarters, lengthways, and arrange on serving plates. Drizzle with a little extra virgin olive oil and spoon the tapenade to one side.

Black Olive Tapenade *(makes 350 ml)*
5oz (150g) Black Olives *(stoned)*
8 Anchovy Fillets
2½oz (60 g) Capers *(drained and washed)*
2 Garlic Cloves *(peeled)*
½ Dessertspoon Thyme *(dried)*
½ Cup (125 ml) Olive Oil
Juice of ¼ Lemon
Ground Black Pepper

Put olives, anchovy fillets, capers, garlic and thyme into a food processor. Keep motor running and drizzle olive oil in to form a paste. Add lemon juice and pepper to taste - store in the fridge.

 Remember, don't add salt as the anchovies are really salty!

Tiger Prawns Pan-fried in Garlic Butter
with White Wine and Spring Onions
(serves 4)

*If you can't get your hands on fresh prawns don't worry
about using frozen, but make sure they are completely
defrosted before you start.*

INGREDIENTS:
2 Tablespoons Black Olives
5oz (150g) Butter
½ Lemon
1 Garlic Clove *(finely chopped)*
5 Spring Onions *(sliced)*
1 Glass Dry White Wine
16 Tiger Prawns
Sea Salt & Ground Black Pepper

First melt the butter in a frying pan then add the white wine,
seasoning and garlic.

Allow to cook gently for 2-3 minutes until you have a light
creamy colour, then add prawns and olives.

Keep turning the prawns in the liquid and cook for 4-5 minutes.
*(Do not reduce the sauce by too much as this is an important part
of the finished dish, you can always add a splash of white wine if
needed.)*

Just before serving add spring onions and squeeze in the lemon
juice.

Serve with chunky pieces of bread to soak up the delightful
flavours.

Warming Mediterranean Avocados

(serves 6)

*While there are a multitude of ways to prepare avocados
as cold starters, this is an alternative which makes a
lovely hot start to a meal on those cold wintry nights.*

INGREDIENTS:

3 Avocados *(slightly under-ripe is ideal)*
Pinch of Fenugreek or Cardamom Seeds
2oz (50g) Lightly Toasted Cashew Nuts
(break down slightly in a food processor)
2oz (50g) Breadcrumbs *(See page 30)*
8oz (225g) Mixed Peppers *(finely chopped)*
2oz (50g) Olives *(stoned, roughly chopped)*
Pinch of Turmeric
Small Bunch of Fresh Coriander Leaves
½ Garlic Clove *(crushed)*
½ Lemon
1 Dessertspoon Balsamic Wine Vinegar
2 Dessertspoons Olive Oil
Salt & Ground Black Pepper

Cut the avocados in half *(lengthways)*, scoop the flesh out and
slice into small cubes then place in a mixing bowl - set aside.
Squeeze some of the lemon juice into the avocado skins and rub
around to prevent them from discolouring, then set aside.
Heat the oil in a pan and gently fry the fenugreek to release the
flavour then remove. Then add to the pan the mixed peppers,
garlic, cashew nuts, olives, breadcrumbs, turmeric and seasoning -
mix thoroughly and cook gently for 5 minutes.
Lastly add the coriander, splash in the Balsamic Wine Vinegar
and squeeze in the rest of the lemon juice and transfer to the
mixing bowl. Mix with the avocado flesh and spoon into skins,
then bake in a medium oven (180°C / Gas Mark 4) for 15 minutes.

Seared Fresh Chicken Livers

(serves 4)

*Liver Pâtés and Terrines are so popular that we have created an
alternative way of cooking chicken livers.*
*Make sure the livers are bright looking and feel springy to the
touch. Keep refrigerated before using.*

INGREDIENTS:

1lb (450g) Fresh Chicken Livers
6 Shallots *(sliced)*
2oz (50g) Lightly Toasted Pine Nuts
Small Bunch Fresh Tarragon and Coriander Leaves
A Handful of French Bread Crôutons
2 Tablespoons Balsamic Wine Vinegar
2 Tablespoons Marsala Wine
2 Tablespoons Clear Honey
½ Garlic Clove *(crushed)*
1 Iceberg Lettuce *(cut into quarters*
then half each quarter horizontally)
1 Tablespoon Chicken Stock *(see page 29)* **or Water**
2 Tablespoons Olive Oil
Coarse Sea Salt

Heat the oil in a large frying pan until hot. Add the livers and seal
fiercely. Add the shallots, garlic and pine nuts. Drizzle in the
honey then add seasoning, Balsamic Wine Vinegar, Marsala and
stock. Allow to reduce for 1 minute then add fresh herbs.
Transfer to a mixing bowl, add lettuce leaves and crôutons and
mix gently so you don't break the livers. Portion on to main
course plates pulling the lettuce up for height. Serve immediately.

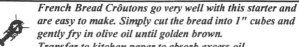

*French Bread Crôutons go very well with this starter and
are easy to make. Simply cut the bread into 1" cubes and
gently fry in olive oil until golden brown.
Transfer to kitchen paper to absorb excess oil.*

Kimshi

(Serves 4)

We're really not too sure if this is a formal name for a recipe, but it was inspired by an incredible starter we enjoyed in a Chinese noodle shack. They had used shelled tiger prawns - however, it would work equally as well with scallops, monkfish, salmon or even mackerel.

INGREDIENTS:

Juice of 12 Limes
2½oz (65g) Leeks *(white part thinly sliced)*
2½oz (65g) Green Peppers *(thinly sliced)*
2½oz (65g) Red Peppers *(thinly sliced)*
2½oz (65g) Fresh Root Ginger *(thinly sliced)*
1 Teaspoon of Orange Blossom Water
2 Oranges
(with a sharp knife peel the oranges, remove all the pith and cut into segments)
1 Glass Dry White Wine
1 Level Tablespoon of Chopped Fresh Coriander
1 Level Teaspoon Coarse Sea Salt
1 Dessertspoon Clear Honey
Choice of Filleted Fresh Fish - approx 1lb (500g)

Mix all the ingredients to make a marinade. Pour half of it into a bowl and sit the fish on top. Then pour on the rest of the marinade, making sure the fish is completely covered.
Place cling wrap over the top and allow to "cure" for a minimum of 24 hours in a refrigerator, turning the fish occasionally.
Serve with crispy greens or fresh Chinese noodles *(cold)*.

 "Curing." The acidic lime juice pickles and tenderises the fish so that it does not require cooking.

Greek Village Salad

(Serves 4)

A meal in Greece isn't quite the same without their traditional salad. This is our version - a perfect starter, but with extra olive oil and crusty bread, it makes a lovely light lunch.

INGREDIENTS:

2 Medium Onions *(thickly sliced)*
2 Beef Tomatoes *(cut into chunks)*
½ Cucumber *(peel skin off and cut into oblong shapes)*
1 Small Packet of Greek Feta Cheese
1 Tablespoon Black Olives
1 Tablespoon Green Olives
1 Level Teaspoon Dried Oregano
A Few Leaves of Fresh Basil
1 Lemon for Squeezing
½ Cup Good Quality Greek Olive Oil
(Kalamata is exceptional!)

Slice the Feta, then mix it together with the rest of the ingredients, being careful not to break it up.

Be careful when you're buying Feta cheese to make sure it is of GREEK origin. You may be surprised how much Feta cheese is made in Holland for example. Keep it truly authentic!

Pan-fried Garlic Mushrooms
with Tarragon and Cream

(Serves 4)

*We seem to have an affinity with mushrooms, which
are always very popular on our menus. They are a
wonderful accompaniment with most foods but
here's a recipe for them to be enjoyed on their own.*

INGREDIENTS:
1 Level Teaspoon Spanish Paprika
24oz (700g) Fresh White Button Mushrooms
4oz (100g) Butter
1 Dessertspoon Dijon Mustard
1 Small Bunch Fresh Tarragon *(removed from stalks)*
2 Garlic Cloves *(crushed)*
Salt & Ground Black Pepper
8fl oz (250ml) Single Cream
½ Glass Dry White Wine

Heat the butter in a pan and sauté the mushrooms for 2-3 minutes
until they begin to take some colour.
Add mustard, seasoning, garlic, paprika and mix together. Add
the wine, simmer gently and allow to reduce.
Add the tarragon and cream and simmer for 2-3 minutes.
Delightful!

*Why not pick up a small packet of wild mushrooms and
add them as well - you will be surprised at the additional
flavours they offer!*

Smoked Salmon and Mussel Broth

(serves 4 - 6)

*Often in supermarkets you'll come across small bags of
"Smoked Salmon Offcuts". These are simply the pieces
which are too small to be sold in sleeves of smoked
salmon but in taste terms are exactly the same
product at a much reduced price!*

INGREDIENTS:

6oz (175g) Smoked Salmon Pieces
4 Dozen Fresh Mussels *(for cleaning see page 11)*
4 Tomatoes *(roughly chopped)*
8oz (225g) Cooked Potatoes *(skinned & roughly chopped)*
1 Large Onion *(roughly chopped)*
4 Shallots *(roughly chopped)*
Salt and Ground Black Pepper
1 Dessertspoon Tomato Purée
3oz (75g) Butter
1 Level Teaspoon Turmeric
1½pts (900ml) Fish Stock *(see page 29)*
2fl oz (60ml) Fresh Cream

Gently fry the onion and shallots in butter until just transparent
(keep the crunch in them!) then add the turmeric, tomato purée
and seasoning. Stir and fry for one minute. Add everything else,
except the mussels, and simmer for 15 minutes. Finally add the
mussels and allow 2-3 mins. for them to cook through *(when the
shells open the mussels are ready)*. Serve the soup arranging the
mussels around the outside of the bowl and finish off with a swirl
of double cream.

Chilled Spanish Water Melon with Minted Oranges

(serves 4 - 6 or 1 person for a week!)

Sometimes it seems that we over complicate things when entertaining, probably feeling that the more complex a meal the better it will be - WHY?

This starter is perfect if you want to be a little more adventurous with your main course and will take a lot of the pressure off. Just be sure to buy the best quality fruit.

INGREDIENTS:
1 Water Melon *(chilled)*
8 Oranges
Bunch of Fresh Mint

Cut the water melon in half. Lay the flat surface face down and cut it through the middle again. Then cut your slices into large smiles - arrange on a large serving dish.

Next remove the skin and pith from the oranges and cut out the orange segments - simply cut between the skin.

Place the segments in a bowl and squeeze the remaining juice from the skin over them.

Chop some fresh mint and mix into the orange segments. *(If you feel you'd like more orange juice cut another one in half and squeeze out the juice)* .

Pour the orange segments over the water melon and serve.

 For a refreshing addition cut 4 passion fruits in half, scoop the contents into the bowl of orange segments and mix together.

Brian's Tomato and Red Pepper Soup

(serves 6)

"There's no show without Punch" and our chef Brian couldn't be left out. This is his recipe although we're sure we must have been its inspiration somewhere along the line!!

INGREDIENTS:

1 Medium Onion *(roughly chopped)*
2 Red Peppers *(remove green stalk, chop in half, but leave seeds in)*
3 Tablespoons Tomato Purée
2 Garlic Cloves *(chopped)*
Salt and Ground Black Pepper
1½ pts (900 ml) Chicken Stock *(see page 29)*
Small Bunch Fresh Coriander Leaves
2lbs (900g) Peeled Plum Tomatoes *(chopped)*
2fl oz (60 ml) Cream
2oz (50g) Fresh Chives *(chopped)*

Sauté onions and peppers until soft then add in the garlic, seasoning and tomato purée.
Pour in the stock, coriander and plum tomatoes, bring to the boil and simmer for 1 hour.
Then purée in a food processor and reheat gently in a pan.
Serve with a swirl of cream and chopped chives.

 Don't remove the seeds of the peppers. They will add character to the finished soup.

Portuguese-Style Sardines

(serves 2)
Relive the magic of your Portuguese holiday!

INGREDIENTS:
6 Large Sardines
Sifted Plain Flour to Coat
Spanish Paprika
1 Lemon for Squeezing
2 Tablespoons Olive Oil *(good quality!)*

Heat the olive oil in a pan large enough to take all the fish. Place the sardines into the flour, shake off the excess and add to the hot oil.
Fry on each side for a couple of minutes, until crisp and golden.
Transfer to a serving dish, squeeze with lemon juice and dust with paprika.

 An authentic alternative would be to sprinkle the fish with sea salt and paprika and cook over charcoal.

Steamed Haggis with a Drambuie, Cream & Grainy Mustard Sauce

(serves 4)

You don't get much more traditional than this! What's nice about steaming the haggis is that it keeps it very moist.

INGREDIENTS:
1lb (450g) Haggis
1 Dessertspoon Olive Oil
6 Shallots *(thinly sliced)*
2 Dessertspoons Grainy Mustard
1 Tablespoon Drambuie
1 cup (200 ml) Single Cream
Salt
2oz (50g) Butter

Take four ramekin pots and rub the inside lightly with the oil *(this stops the haggis sticking)*.

Push the haggis into each ramekin and press down firmly - *if you don't have ramekin pots don't worry, coffee cups will do.*

Place in a steamer and allow ten minutes to warm through.

Meanwhile make the sauce as follows -

Melt the butter in a pan and add the shallots and salt.

Cook until the shallots are transparent then add the grainy mustard. Move around the pan until the base is covered then add the Drambuie. Allow to flambé and when the flames subside pour in the cream. Mix to a rich consistency.

Turn the Haggis pots upside down on the serving plates and spoon the sauce over the top.

Slàinte!!

 Steamers are readily available, and inexpensive, at most good Chinese supermarkets.

MAIN COURSES

3 Basic Home-made Stocks
Breast of Chicken, Butter and Lemon
Brochette of Monkfish
Mediterranean Stuffed Peppers
Courgette & Chicken Tortilla
Moroccan Lamb Tagine
Sheftalia
Savoury Crêpes
Fresh Seafood Crêpes
Spanish Knuckle of Chicken
Pasta Tossed through a Fresh Tomato and Basil
Sauce
Wild Mushroom Risotto
Spiced Fillets of Beef with Chillis
Bruschetta
Mediterranean Oven-Baked Sea Bass
Portuguese Chicken "Piri-Piri"
Hungarian Beef Goulash

Home Made Stocks

There are all sorts of stock cubes to be bought off the shelf but there really is no substitute for making your own and they're easier to make than you may think. Here are some simple steps to follow to make three different stocks using the same basic ingredients.

Common Ingredients:
6pts (3.6lts) Cold Water
1 Onion *(cut in half - keep skin on)*
2 Clean Carrots *(cut into 1" cubes)*
1 Teaspoon Coarse Sea Salt
1 Stick Celery *(roughly chopped)*
6 Whole Black Peppercorns
1 Leek *(washed and cut into 1" lengths)*

<u>Fish Stock</u> - 2lbs mixed Fish Bones *(not oily fish e.g. Mackerel)*

<u>Chicken Stock</u> - 2lbs Chicken Bones/Carcasses

<u>Vegetable Stock</u> - Double the quantities of vegetables and add a handful of fresh herbs.

Add everything to the pot, put on a high heat and bring through the boil. Reduce the heat and allow to simmer gently for half an hour. *(The chicken stock should be allowed to simmer for about 1½ hours)* Skim the top and remove bones/vegetables.
Pass through a fine strainer and put back onto the heat.
Allow to reduce, to concentrate the flavours, then allow to cool.

Stocks can be made in bulk then frozen, but remember don't freeze in bulk. Small tinfoil fast food containers are ideal to freeze smaller amounts of stock which can then be used as needed - remember to mark on top what kind of stock is in each container!

Breast of Chicken, Butter & Lemon

(serves 2)

This really is one of the simplest main courses imaginable, it makes an excellent light meal and is very quick to prepare.

INGREDIENTS:
2 Chicken Breasts
2oz (50g) Breadcrumbs
4oz (100g) Butter
¼ Lemon
½ Glass of Dry White Wine
1 Beaten Egg

Dip the chicken breasts in the beaten egg and coat with breadcrumbs.

Melt half the butter in a frying pan and add the chicken breasts. Move the chicken around in the pan and turn over when just beginning to brown *(2-3 minutes)* and repeat for the other side.

Remove from the heat and place in an oven-proof dish.

Squeeze lemon juice over the chicken and add the rest of the butter and wine.

Season and bake *(uncovered)* in a medium oven (180° C / Gas Mark 4) for 20 minutes or until ready.

MAKE YOUR OWN BREADCRUMBS

Cut a loaf of your favourite crusty bread into slices and leave on an open roasting tray for 2-3 days until hard. Place into a food processor and whizz until very fine. Rub through a sieve and store the fine crumbs in a jar. Don't discard what's left in the sieve - you've just made rough breadcrumbs as well!

Brochette of Monkfish

(serves 4)

A "Brochette" is simply a skewer or spit.
The name has a certain ring about it and sounds great if
you want to impress your guests - keep this one for when
you're entertaining "The Boss!"

INGREDIENTS:

1½lb (675g) Monkfish Tail Fillets *(cut to 1" cubes)*
6oz (175g) Chorizo Sausages *(sliced to ½" thick)*
1 Green Pepper *(cut into 1" squares)*
1 Yellow Pepper *(cut into 1" squares)*
1 Red Pepper *(cut into 1" squares)*
1 Lemon for Squeezing
Olive Oil

Make up the skewers by threading the monkfish, Chorizo and
peppers alternately along the length of the skewer.
Squeeze the lemon over the brochettes.
Drizzle a touch of olive oil on the base of an oven-proof dish,
add the brochettes and cook until the fish becomes white on the
outside *(about 20 minutes in a moderate oven - 180°C / Gas
Mark 4)* - turn them after 10 minutes to ensure even cooking.
Simply serve with crispy salad and savoury rice.

 Don't forget Brochettes are great cooked on the BBQ.

Mediterranean Stuffed Peppers

(serves 6)

*This is a great way of using up all those bits & pieces
that seem to accumulate in our fridges.*

INGREDIENTS:

8 Tomatoes *(roughly chopped)*
12oz (350g) Button Mushrooms *(thinly sliced)*
2oz (50g) Halloumi Cheese *(finely chopped)*
2oz (50g) Feta Cheese *(crumbled)*
1 Small Bunch Fresh Basil Leaves
1 Small Bunch Fresh Coriander Leaves
Juice of ½ Lemon
½ Garlic Clove *(crushed)*
1 Level Teaspoon Cumin Powder
1 Tablespoon Capers *(drained and washed)*
1 Tablespoon Olives *(stoned)*
Salt and Ground Black Pepper
4 Tablespoons Olive Oil
6oz (175g) Rough Breadcrumbs *(see page 30)*
6 Medium Red Peppers

Cut the peppers in half *(lengthways)* and remove the seeds - *try to
cut right through the stalk and leave it on the pepper.*
Put all of the above ingredients in a large bowl, except the
breadcrumbs, and mix together with four tablespoons of olive oil.
Spoon the mixture into each of the pepper halves and sprinkle the
rough breadcrumbs on top.
Bake in a moderate oven (180°C / Gas Mark 4) for approx 25
mins until the crumbs are lightly browned on top.

Courgette and Chicken Tortilla

(serves 4 - 6)
Spanish Tortillas are very versatile.
Serve them as a hot main meal or allow them to cool
and take them on a picnic.

INGREDIENTS:

12oz (350g) Cooked Potatoes *(finely cubed)*
1 Medium Onion *(finely chopped)*
1 Chicken Breast *(finely chopped)*
6 Small Courgettes *(thinly sliced)*
8 Eggs *(beaten)*
Pinch of Cayenne Pepper
1 Small Bunch Fresh Herbs *(Coriander/Flat Leaf Parsley)*
6 Spring Onions *(finely chopped)*
2oz (50g) Butter
1 Garlic Clove *(crushed)*
Salt and Ground Black Pepper

Melt the butter in a large frying pan and sauté the onions and garlic until softened.

Add the chicken pieces and cook for a further 5 minutes.

Add the potatoes and sprinkle with seasoning and cayenne pepper. Mix everything together with a wooden spoon and add the sliced courgettes, spring onions and herbs. Then add the beaten eggs. Allow to simmer gently until the base sets, then put the pan under a hot grill and cook the tortilla until set and firm to the touch. Slide on to a chopping board and cut into wedges.

The secret of success with Tortillas is to use a very well oiled pan to avoid sticking and not to overcook the eggs.

Moroccan Lamb Tagine

(Serves 10 - 12)

*A "Tagine" is simply a casserole and therefore is less intimidating than a lot of dishes. What's nice about this recipe is that everything is mixed together **before** you start cooking then all you need to do is cover it and pop it into the oven! This is ideal if you're entertaining a larger number of friends, it's **"hassle-free"**.*

INGREDIENTS:

4lb (1.75kg) Gigot Lamb *(cut into large cubes)*
2 Large Onions *(roughly chopped)*
1 Bunch of Fresh Coriander Leaves *(roughly chopped)*
2 Garlic Cloves *(crushed)*
12oz (350g) Dried Apricots *(roughly chopped)*
2 Tins Coconut Milk
½ Bottle Full Bodied Red Wine *(Not Plonk!)*
½ Jar Clear Honey (230g)
2 Heaped Tablespoons Tomato Purée
4 Medium Tomatoes *(roughly chopped, skin on is OK)*
2 Tablespoons Lightly Toasted Cashew Nuts
Sea Salt and Ground Black Pepper
1 Dessertpoon each of Turmeric, Cumin and Coriander

Put all the ingredients into a large bowl and mix thoroughly. *For best results use your hands.*

Transfer to a casserole dish and cover tightly with tinfoil. Place into a preheated oven (150°C / Gas Mark 2) and cook gently for about three hours. Serve with rice and pitta bread.

An alternative to tinned Coconut Milk is Creamed Coconut. Break the contents of 2 packets (396g in total) into a heat-proof bowl, add 1½ pints boiling water and leave to settle for 15 mins. Whisk thoroughly to ensure a smooth consistency.

Sheftalia

(serves 2)

Sheftalia are meatballs which can either be pan-fried, open-roasted in the oven or are fantastic skewered and cooked over charcoal. To help the meat bind really well ask your butcher to put it through the mincer 4 times or whizz it in a food processor until really fine.

INGREDIENTS:

8oz (225g) Minced Lamb
8oz (225g) Minced Pork
1 Level Teaspoon Dried Mint
1 Level Teaspoon Dried Oregano
1 Level Teaspoon Paprika
1 Level Teaspoon Turmeric
1 Garlic Clove *(chopped)*
Squeeze of Lemon Juice
Salt and Ground Black Pepper

Place all of the above ingredients into a large mixing bowl and mix thoroughly.

Separate into individual balls of approx. 2oz (50g) each and roll them between your hands.

Drizzle some olive oil on the base of a roasting dish.

Place the sheftalia on top and open roast in a moderate oven (180°C / Gas Mark 4) until cooked *(approx 20 minutes)* turning occasionally.

Serve on a traditional Greek Village Salad *(see page 19)*

 If cooking over charcoal, soak wooden skewers in water overnight to prevent them from burning, then thread on the sheftalia.

Savoury Crêpes

There's something very rewarding about making your own crêpes. They can be enjoyed with a variety of fillings. Don't just save them for pancake day!

INGREDIENTS:

4oz (100g) Sifted Plain Flour
Pinch of Salt
8fl oz (250ml) Milk
2 Whole Eggs
3 Teaspoons Olive Oil
½ Measure Brandy

Put the eggs, salt, olive oil and brandy into a food processor and whizz together until smooth and frothy. Sift the flour into a large mixing bowl and make a hole in the middle. Slowly add the mixture and fold together pulling the flour in from the sides of the bowl. You should end up with a thick paste. Now slowly drizzle in the milk, beating constantly, until you have a consistently smooth batter. Allow to settle for one hour. *The secret of success when making crêpes is to have a dedicated crêpe pan and to make sure you have everything at hand before you start.* Warm the pan and add a teaspoon of oil. When it begins to smoke pour the excess off. Pour enough batter to thinly cover the bottom of the pan, swirl around and don't be afraid to pour any excess back. Allow to brown slightly then turn over using a palette knife. Brown the other side and transfer to a plate. Wipe the pan with a dry clean cloth and repeat the process. Stack the crêpes, layering with greaseproof paper. Crêpes freeze very well so don't be afraid to make a batch and store them in the freezer.

 Sometimes, if you've had distractions, your batter may not end up as smooth as you would have liked. CHEAT!! but don't tell anyone. Pass it through a sieve and bin the evidence!

Fresh Seafood Crêpes

This is a wonderful way to enjoy filleted fish or shellfish but requires some forward planning. First make the filling - a seafood chowder, then make the crêpes. (See opposite page)

INGREDIENTS FOR FILLING:

2 Carrots *(grated)*
2 Sticks Celery *(roughly chopped)*
1 Medium Onion *(roughly chopped)*
2 Garlic Cloves *(crushed)*
1 Tablespoon Tomato Purée
1 Teaspoon Turmeric
1 Teaspoon Spanish Paprika
1 Teaspoon Dill
1 Teaspoon Fennel Seeds
Juice of ½ Lemon
2pts (1.25lts) Fish Stock *(see page 29)*
1lb (450g) Selected Fresh Raw Fish *(roughly cut)*
3oz (75g) Butter
Salt and Ground Black Pepper

Melt butter in a pot *(large enough to take all the ingredients)* and sauté carrots, celery, onions and garlic for 3-4 minutes. Add the tomato purée and stir well in. Add fish stock, spices, fennel seeds, dill, lemon juice and seasoning. Bring through the boil and allow to simmer for 10 minutes, then add all the raw fish, boil again and allow to simmer for 5 minutes. Remove from heat and allow to cool. Then place a crêpe on your board, spoon in some of the cold fish filling, straining off any excess liquid and roll into a cigar shape. For each portion allow three crêpes and feel free to sprinkle a little grated Gruyère cheese on top. Cover with tinfoil and bake in a moderate oven (180° C / Gas Mark 4) for 10 minutes. Remove tinfoil and bake for a further 5 minutes until the cheese melts.

Spanish Knuckle of Chicken

(serves 6 - 8)

This is a fantastic, colourful, flavoursome casserole dish which is an economical "centre-of-the-table" affair when entertaining friends informally. If you're not happy jointing the chicken yourself speak nicely to your butcher - keep the skin on to add to the authenticity and style of the dish.

INGREDIENTS:

3½lb (1.5kg) Chicken
(once jointed, chop the legs & thighs in half)
2 Red Onions *(quartered)*
2 Stalks Celery *(cut into 1" chunks)*
3 Peppers
(medium size, red, green & yellow - roughly chopped)
1 Lemon for Squeezing
½ Bottle Dry White Wine
8 Medium Tomatoes *(quartered)*
2 Garlic Cloves *(crushed)*
6 Mushrooms *(halved)*
Bunch of Fresh Herbs *(sage, basil, rosemary)*
3 Tablespoons of Olive Oil
1 Level Dessertspoon Spanish Paprika
2 Heaped Tablespoons Black Olives *(stoned)*
Salt and Ground Black Pepper
2 Medium Sized Courgettes *(cut into ½" thick slices)*
4 Spicy Chorizo Sausages *(cut into ½" thick slices)*
2½pts (1.55lts) Chicken Stock *(see page 29)*

Before you start, decide on an oven-proof dish that will be large enough to take all of the ingredients and the liquid!

Heat 2 tablespoons of olive oil in a frying pan and seal the chicken pieces *(be sure to brown both sides but beware of any "spitting" from the pan. You may have to do this in batches - don't overcrowd the pan.)*

When sealed transfer to the casserole dish.

In a clean frying pan heat a tablespoon of olive oil and add peppers, onions, garlic, celery and seasoning.

Gently simmer the vegetables until they begin to take a little colour then add tomatoes, mushrooms, paprika and herbs.

Mix thoroughly and transfer to the casserole dish.

Add wine, chicken stock *(make your own see page 29)*, lemon juice and olives and cover with a tightfitting lid or tinfoil.

Cook gently in a moderate oven (180°C / Gas Mark 4) for 1 hour.

Remove from the oven then add Chorizo and courgettes and mix through. Return casserole to the oven for 15 minutes, then serve directly with piles of your favourite bread for "Dunking"!

 If you need to extend this dish out a bit add either cooked potatoes or pasta when the Chorizo sausages and courgettes go in. For colour when placing your "masterpiece" in the middle of the table, add a few lemon wedges (skin side up) and a few sprigs of fresh rosemary on top!

Pasta Tossed through a Fresh Tomato and Basil Sauce

(serves 6)

This is one of those fabulously rustic sauces which is a classic base for all kinds of variations. Once it's made it can either be served on its own or extended by adding other ingredients (e.g. spicy sausages)

INGREDIENTS:

3 Medium Sized Onions *(roughly chopped)*
3 Tablespoons Tomato Purée
4 Garlic Cloves *(chopped)*
1 Teaspoon Dried Oregano
2 x 400g Tins Chopped Plum Tomatoes
Salt and Ground Black Pepper
A Handful of Fresh Basil *(roughly chopped)*
2 Tablespoons Olive Oil
1¼lbs (500g) Fresh or Dried Pasta
(cooked until "al dente")

Gently fry the onions in olive oil until transparent then add garlic, tomato purée, oregano and seasoning and when thoroughly mixed together add tomatoes and fresh basil and simmer gently for 20 minutes.

When ready add the cooked pasta, mix together and serve right away with freshly grated Parmesan cheese and a bowl of crispy lettuce leaves.

 "Al dente" can make or break the success of any pasta and describes the stage it is cooked to when there is still a slight bite in the pasta.

Wild Mushroom Risotto

(serves 4 - 6)

You can buy wild mushrooms loose or in small boxes which usually contain 4-5 different types. This is probably the best idea because it offers a nice variety of flavours. If you have a paella pan it would be perfect for cooking the risotto.

INGREDIENTS:

1lb (450g) Arborio Rice *(round grain rice)*
12oz (350g) Wild and Button Mushrooms
(roughly chopped)
1 Medium Onion *(finely chopped)*
1 Garlic Clove *(crushed)*
2 Teaspoons Dijon Mustard
2oz (50g) Butter
2 Tablespoons Olive Oil
Salt and Ground Black Pepper
Small Bunch of Fresh Tarragon Leaves
2-3pts (1-2lts) Vegetable Stock *(see page 29)*

Warm the butter and olive oil in a large pan over a moderate heat, add the onions and soften for 2-3 minutes. Add garlic and seasoning to taste then add the rice - stir thoroughly.

Keep "agitating" the rice with a wooden spoon and just as it is beginning to colour (lightly golden) add enough hot stock to cover and stir in the Dijon mustard.

Just before all the liquid evaporates add the mushrooms and tarragon then more stock to barely cover.

You must continuously stir and test the rice until "al dente" adding more stock when required.

 The risotto should be "sticky" without too much liquid, so it is probably better to add small amounts of liquid at a time.

Spiced Fillets of Beef with Chillis

(serves 6)

This is a dish which requires you to be there from start to finish - true á la carte cooking, so make sure you have everything at hand before you start. It requires the prime cut of beef, anything less just won't do.

INGREDIENTS:

2lbs (900g) Fillet Steak *(cut into 2" cubes)*
9 Shallots *(cut in half then into wedges)*
1 Large Red Pepper *(cut into ½" fingers)*
1 Tablespoon Tomato Purée
1 Garlic Clove *(crushed)*
1 Dessertspoon Fresh Root Ginger *(thinly sliced)*
1 Fresh Chilli *(thinly sliced)*
1 Dessertspoon of Brandy
1 Dessertspoon of Marsala Wine
1 Glass Rich Red Wine
1 Cup of Water
1 Tablespoon Olive Oil
Sea Salt and Ground Black Pepper

Heat the oil in a large frying pan. Add the beef and sear fiercely until browned all over. Add the red peppers and shallots and stir well. Then add the tomato purée; just as it begins to stick throw in the brandy and Marsala and allow to flame *(watch your eyebrows!)*. When the flames have subsided add water, garlic, ginger, chilli and seasoning.

Allow to simmer and when you have a nice rich consistency serve immediately with either rice, noodles or pasta.

 If you prefer your beef well done cut the beef cubes in half before you start cooking. If you prefer your beef rare transfer to a dish when sealed and keep warm. Finish off making the sauce then add the beef just before serving.

Bruschetta

(serves 6 - or 4 hungry Horaces!)

Apparently the concept for this "peasants lunch" came from the Italian farmers' fields when they would warm their bread over a fire and add ham and cheese on the top! You have complete poetic licence with the ingredients but here we have a guaranteed combination of flavours for success!!

INGREDIENTS:

1 Loaf Crusty Bread *(baguettes are ideal)*
Small Bunch of Fresh Coriander Leaves
Small Bunch of Fresh Basil Leaves
8 Anchovy Fillets *(chopped)*
6 Ripe Tomatoes *(finely diced)*
1 Tablespoon Tomato Purée
6 Slices Air-cured Ham *(either Italian Parma or Spanish Serrano)*
1 Garlic Clove
1 Teaspoon of Dried Oregano
8oz (225g) Mozzarella Cheese *(sliced)*
Ground Sea Salt & Black Pepper
Virgin Olive Oil

Slice the baguette lengthways along the middle. Place cut side down on a chopping board and slightly flatten with a rolling pin. Turn over and cut the garlic clove in half then rub along the cut surface of the bread. Spread the tomato purée evenly *(not too thickly)* along both sides. Cut the baguette sides into 3 equal lengths to give 6 portions. Now mix all the other ingredients except the ham together and moisten with olive oil. Place a slice of ham on to each base and evenly spread the filling on top. Cover each with cheese and bake in a moderate oven (180°C / Gas Mark 4) for 15 to 20 minutes or until golden on top. To serve sprinkle with a little dried oregano.

Mediterranean Oven-baked Sea Bass

(serves 4)

This is a wonderful way of serving whole fish and really couldn't be easier to make. The combination of flavours in the sauce permeates through the fish whilst cooking.

INGREDIENTS:
4 Whole Fresh Sea Bass
*(scaled, gutted and lightly criss-crossed,
just enough to break the skin)*

Ingredients for the Sauce:
6 Tomatoes *(roughly chopped)*
1 Garlic Clove *(roughly chopped)*
Juice of ½ Lemon
2 Dessertspoons Black Olives *(stoned)*
1 Dessertspoon Capers *(drained and washed)*
1 Level Teaspoon Cumin
1 Level Teaspoon Turmeric
2 Glasses Dry White Wine
½ Teaspoon Fennel Seeds
Coarse Sea Salt
1 Small Bunch Fresh Coriander Leaves
1 Small Bunch Fresh Dill

Mix all of the above ingredients together and pour on to the bottom of an oven-proof dish.

Sit the fish directly on top, pushing any of the exposed sauce underneath the sea bass, sprinkle liberally with sea salt, and bake *(uncovered)* in the oven (180°C /Gas Mark 4) for approx 25 minutes until the fish is ready.

Place the casserole dish on a board in the centre of the table so that everyone can enjoy the aromas, then serve.

Portuguese Chicken "Piri-Piri"

(serves 2)

*This is our interpretation of the ubiquitous spicy
Portuguese sauce which can go with almost anything -
Fish, Beef, Lamb, Vegetables etc. etc. Here we've chosen
chicken and although we've made WADS of sauce don't
paste it all on, jar it and it'll keep for ages in the fridge!*

INGREDIENTS:
2 Legs & 2 Thighs Chicken
(Keep the skin on but score the flesh)

FOR THE "PIRI-PIRI":
3 Dessertspoons Dried Chillis
Juice of 1 Lemon
1 Dessertspoon Brandy
3 Dessertspoons Soy Sauce
½ Jar Clear Honey (230g)
1 Glass Red Wine *(Rich Red not Plonko!)*
1 Cup (200ml) Olive Oil
2 Dessertspoons Tomato Purée
Ground Sea Salt & Black Pepper
Juice of ½ Orange
¼ Onion *(chopped)*
2 Garlic Cloves *(chopped)*
1 Medium Red Pepper *(chopped)*

Blend all the above ingredients for the sauce until you have a
smooth paste. Sit the chicken pieces on an oven-proof dish, *(skin
side up)* and paint the paste on top. Put a touch of water to just
cover the base of the dish so the chicken doesn't stick, and bake in
a moderate oven (180°C / Gas Mark 4) until cooked *(approx. 35
mins)*. Serve with a cooling salad and plain boiled potatoes.

 *If you like your chicken very hot, instead of scoring, cut the
flesh through to the bone and slap the paste into the meat!*

Hungarian Beef Goulash

(serves 4)

This is one of these robust casserole dishes - not for the faint hearted! When the wind's blowing and it's cold and wintry outside add a glow to your evening and throw a few extra chillis in - you'll not feel the cold for days!!

<u>INGREDIENTS:</u>

1½ lb (675g) Beef *(cut into large chunks)*
1 Large Onion *(thickly sliced)*
6 Tomatoes *(roughly chopped)*
2 Fresh Chillis *(finely sliced)*
1 Teaspoon Caraway Seeds
1 Dessertspoon Spanish Paprika
Salt and Ground Black Pepper
2 Red Peppers *(cut into chunky pieces)*
1 Garlic Clove *(crushed)*
1pt (600ml) Red Wine *(good quality)*
1½pts (900ml) Water
4 Tablespoons Vegetable Oil
1 Dessertspoon Tomato Purée

Heat oil in a large frying pan and seal the beef pieces until browned all over. Add onions and peppers and cook for 1-2 minutes then add tomato purée.

Move everything around the pan and just before the purée begins to stick, add tomatoes, red wine, water, chillis, garlic and spices. Put into an oven-proof dish and cover with tinfoil.

Cook in a moderate oven (180°C / Gas Mark 4) for 1½ hours until ready.

The Goulash can either be served right away or allowed to cool, refrigerated and re-heated the following day - like any good soup!!

DESSERTS

Raspberry Ice Cream
Banoffi Pie
Strawberry Meringue Syllabub
Peach & Brandy Snap Pudding
Chocolate Meringue Cake
Ice Cream Pudding
Hot Fudge Sundae
Carrot Cake
Baked Cinnamon Oranges
Chocolate Caramel Shortcake
Isobel's Pineapple Cake
Tiramisu
Apple Mincemeat and Marzipan Strudel
Brown Sugar Meringues
Debbie's Butterscotch Sauce

Raspberry Ice Cream

This is so easy - it's a dawdle!

INGREDIENTS:
8oz (225g) Frozen Raspberries
10fl oz (300ml) Double Cream

Put the frozen raspberries into a blender or a food processor
and pour in the double cream.

Whizz for 2 mins until the ice cream is a lovely deep colour of
pink.

Spoon it straight away into some brandy snap baskets, decorate
with some sprigs of fresh mint and serve.

If you have some extra raspberries *(defrosted of course)*, use them
as decoration.

(This sweet looks so impressive, there's no need to tell!!)

*If you can only find brandy snaps instead of the baskets don't
worry. Place them on a baking tray (only a couple at a time)
and pop them into a warm oven for a few minutes.
Gradually they will soften and uncurl.
Using a palette knife, lift them off the tray and place
them over an upturned cup or glass. Drape the sides slightly
around the cup and the basket will harden in minutes.*

Banoffi Pie

(Serves 6)

ABRACADABRA!! Two tins of milk turned into toffee!!

INGREDIENTS:

Biscuit Base : 1 Packet Digestive Biscuits
       4oz (100g) Melted Butter
       1oz (25g) Demerara Sugar

Topping   : 2 Large Tins Condensed Milk (397g each)
       4 Small Bananas

Crush the biscuits, pour in the butter and mix together.

Stir in the demerara sugar and press into a lightly greased 10"
loose bottomed tart tin.

Bake for 10 minutes (150°C / Gas Mark 2) until lightly browned.

Boil <u>unopened</u> tins of condensed milk in a large pan of water for
2½ hours.

***Be careful to keep topping up the water as it boils as the tins
must be covered at all times.***

Remove the tins from the water, allow to cool, open and spread
over the biscuit base.

Peel and slice bananas and arrange them over the toffee, overlap-
ping them slightly.

 *The toffee can also be used as an icing for cakes and
biscuits. It keeps well in a screw topped jar in the fridge.*

Strawberry Meringue Syllabub

(serves 6)

*This is a classic - I think strawberries and
meringues were made for each other.*

INGREDIENTS:
3 Punnets of Strawberries
Juice from 2 Small Oranges
1pt (600ml) Double Cream
2 Tablespoons Cointreau or Orange Liqueur
6 Small Meringues

Slice the strawberries and soak in the orange juice for a few minutes
to bring out the flavour.

Whip the cream with the Cointreau until thickened, but not stiff.

Fold in the crushed meringues and serve in tall glasses layered with
the strained strawberries.

 *Bought meringues are ideal for this as they're easier to
crumble.*

Peach & Brandy Snap Pudding

(Serves 4-6)
*We just love sweets that taste really special but are so
simple to make - this is one of those "make the day before"
puds - try it - you'll soon see why!*

INGREDIENTS:
1pt (600ml) Double Cream
6 - 8 Peaches
1 Packet Brandy Snap Biscuits *(roughly broken)*

Halve the peaches, remove the stones and slice thinly.
Whip the cream lightly until it just starts to thicken.
Add the peach slices and fold in the broken biscuits.
Cover and leave overnight in the fridge for the flavours to
develop.
The Pudding should be slightly darker in colour when ready.
Spoon into glasses and serve.

 *If it's a wee bit too thick when ready to serve, just stir in a
spoonful of cream. Sprinkle on some crushed brandy snaps
to decorate.*

Chocolate Meringue Cake

(Serves 6)

I must admit, everytime meringues appear on our menu they sell extremely quickly, so it's safe to say that you're guaranteed not to have any left over!

INGREDIENTS:

5 Egg Whites
5oz (150g) Demerara Sugar
5oz (150g) Caster Sugar
1 Jar Chocolate Spread (300g)
¾pt (475ml) Double or Whipping Cream
Grated Chocolate *(for decoration)*
Cocoa Powder to Dust

Cover two large baking trays with baking parchment and, using a dinner plate, draw one circle on each tray.

Whisk the egg whites until stiff *(when they start to leave a trail in the mixture)* and then gradually whisk in both sugars.

Fill the circles with the meringue mixture and bake in the oven for 1½ hours (130°C / Gas Mark 1) or until you can safely lift the meringue off the paper.

Allow the meringues to cool, then cover one meringue with the chocolate spread.

Whip the cream until thick and spread half of it on top of the chocolate.

Put the other meringue circle on top and finish with the rest of the cream. Decorate with lots of chocolate shavings and sprinkle with cocoa powder.

 Meringues only work when the egg whites are at room temperature and your kitchen is cool - so open a window, if possible!!

Ice Cream Pudding

(Serves 4)

*Have you ever forgotten to put the ice cream back
into the freezer - don't despair - for your next trick,
a hot ice cream pudding!*

INGREDIENTS:
1 Pint (600ml) Melted Vanilla Ice Cream
1 Beaten Egg
3 Tablespoons Marmalade
4 Trifle Sponges

Whisk the egg into the ice cream and crumble in the sponges.
Spread the marmalade on the base of an ovenproof
casserole dish and pour the ice cream mixture on top.
Bake for approximately 40 minutes (180°C / Gas Mark 4) until
the pudding is set, golden brown on top and the marmalade 'sauce'
is bubbling underneath.

*Always use good quality ice cream for this, which already
contains enough egg yolks to make it set, but I've added an
extra egg, just in case.*

Hot Fudge Sundae

(serves 6 or 4 greedy chocaholics)
Having enjoyed this sundae in America we discovered it's
not all about ice cream and hot fudge sauce. So have
bowls of chopped marshmallows, nuts, grated chocolate,
coconut and dried banana flakes on hand and let everyone
choose their own topping.

INGREDIENTS:
Lots of Vanilla Ice Cream
6oz (175g) Milk or Dark Chocolate
Small Tin of Condensed Milk
1 Cup of Milk

Melt the chocolate with the milk and condensed milk in a double
boiler or in a bowl over simmering water, slowly.
When the sauce melts and becomes thick and gooey, remove from
the heat and spoon over the ice cream which you have scooped
into the largest sundae glasses you can find!

 Don't cheat when it comes to chocolate - always buy the best.

Carrot Cake

(Serves 8)

*Or is it really? With so many other ingredients, I'm not so sure
but this really is "the crème de la crème" of carrot cakes!*

INGREDIENTS:
10oz (275g) Plain Flour
2 Teaspoons Baking Powder
1 Teaspoon Bicarbonate of Soda
½ Teaspoon Grated Nutmeg
1 Teaspoon Cinnamon
3 Eggs
6oz (175g) Soft Brown Sugar
6fl oz (175ml) Sunflower Oil
2 Mashed Bananas
5oz (150g) Grated Carrots
2oz (50g) Chopped Walnuts
2oz (50g) Chopped Dates
ICING:
8oz (225g) Soft Cheese
6oz (175g) Icing Sugar
Zest of 2 Lemons & Juice of 1-2 Lemons

Sieve flour, baking powder and bicarbonate of soda, add nutmeg
and cinnamon. Beat eggs, then fold into the flour mixture
followed by the brown sugar, sunflower oil, bananas, carrots,
walnuts and dates. *(A mixer using a beater is ideal for this)*. Mix
thoroughly and pour into a greased 9" loose bottomed cake tin
lined with greased baking parchment. Bake for approximately 45
minutes (180°C / Gas Mark 4) until a skewer inserted in the centre
of the cake comes out clean. When the cake is cool, mix cheese,
icing sugar and zest together, gradually adding enough lemon
juice until thick enough to spread over the cake.
Decorate with pared orange and lemon zest.

Baked Cinnamon Oranges

(Serves 4)

One of our favourites - can almost follow any meal but allows you to "spice" things up with your favourite tipple!

INGREDIENTS:

4 Oranges *(allow 1 orange per person)*
4 Teaspoons Soft Brown Sugar
4 Tablespoons Orange Liqueur, or Brandy
(or something similar)
4 Cinnamon Sticks

Using a sharp knife, top and tail the oranges and cut away all the skin and pith.

Slice each orange into 4 slices horizontally and secure back together again with two cocktail sticks, making sure they don't pierce the bottom of the orange.

Sit each orange on a large square of tinfoil and sprinkle over the brown sugar, crush the cinnamon stick and pour over the liqueur. Scrunch the tinfoil together above the orange.

Bake the parcels (180°C / Gas Mark 4) for 10 minutes.

 Each guest should receive the 'parcel' intact so that when they open it they can experience the wonderful aroma.

Chocolate Caramel Shortcake

*Also known as "millionaires shortbread" but you don't
have to be a lottery winner to enjoy this old favourite!*

BASE INGREDIENTS:
8oz (225g) Butter
4oz (100g) Caster Sugar
10oz (275g) Plain Flour *(sieved)*

Cream the butter and the sugar in a food processor and add the
flour. Spread this mixture into a lightly greased Swiss roll tin 10 x
7" and bake for 20 minutes (150°C / Gas Mark 2) until golden
brown.

CARAMEL INGREDIENTS:
8oz (225g) Butter
1 Large Tin Condensed Milk (397g)
3 Tablespoons Golden Syrup
8oz (225g) Caster Sugar

Put all these ingredients into a pot and bring to the boil, stirring
continuously. Boil for 5 minutes, still stirring with a wooden
spoon to ensure that the caramel doesn't burn, and pour over the
shortbread base.
Leave to set for 10 minutes.

CHOCOLATE:

Melt 8oz (225g) of good quality chocolate *(milk or plain)* in a
bowl over a pan of simmering water and spread over the caramel.
Before it sets completely, mark into squares.

 *When measuring syrup - heat the tablespoon first and the
syrup will slide off the spoon easily.*

Isobel's Pineapple Cake

My Mum used to make this for any family occasion, in fact it's good enough to serve as a sweet and not just as a cake.

INGREDIENTS:
½ Packet Digestive Biscuits (approx 125g)
2oz (50g) Margarine
1 Egg
4oz (100g) Butter
10oz (275g) Icing Sugar *(sieved)*
10fl oz (300ml) Double Cream
Small Tin Crushed Pineapple
Toasted Coconut

Melt margarine and add to crushed digestive biscuits.
Mix well and press into a Swiss roll tin (10" x 7").
Bake for 10 minutes (150°C / Gas Mark 2) until golden brown and set aside to cool.
Beat the butter and icing sugar together, then add the egg and spread over the cooled biscuit base.
Drain the pineapple, putting the juice into the cream.
Whip the cream and pineapple juice until thickened and fold in the crushed pineapple.
Spread this over the icing mixture and sprinkle with some toasted coconut.
Chill before serving.

 As an alternative to toasted coconut use demerara sugar or chopped nuts.

Tiramisu

(serves 4 - 6)

We all love Tiramisu - but are you still looking for the "Real McCoy?" - well here it is! Laden with calories I know, but you just can't cheat on this one I'm afraid. Enjoy!

INGREDIENTS:
4 Eggs Yolks
5oz (150g) Caster Sugar
4 Tablespoons Marsala Wine
(available from any Italian delicatessen)
9oz (250g) Tub Mascarpone Cheese *(at room temperature)*
8fl oz (250ml) Double Cream
¼pt (150ml) Strong Coffee *(cooled)*
6 Sponge Fingers *(approx 1-1½ fingers per glass)*
Cocoa Powder *(to decorate)*

Put the yolks and sugar in a large bowl over a pan of simmering water, and whisk well. *Use an electric hand held whisk if possible, it's much easier on the arms!*

Gradually whisk in the Marsala and keep whisking for about 5 minutes until the mixture thickens and starts to leave a trail when you lift the mixer.

At this stage, remove from heat and leave to cool, but keep stirring it occasionally.

Now whisk the cream until slightly thickened and pour into a bowl over the softened cheese.

Mix well together, using a hand whisk if necessary, and fold in the cooled egg mixture.

Soak the sponge fingers briefly in the coffee and crumble into the bottom of a glass and cover with the mixture.

Dust with some sieved cocoa powder and chill well before serving.

Apple Mincemeat and Marzipan Strudel

(serves 4)

The wonderful thing about this strudel is that the marzipan melts into the apples and the mincemeat which gives it the most amazing flavour.

INGREDIENTS:

8 Sheets Filo Pastry
2 Apples
2 Tablespoons Mincemeat
1 Squeeze Lemon Juice
2oz (50g) Butter
1 Pinch Cinnamon
2oz (50g) Marzipan *(cut into small cubes)*

Peel and grate the apples, mix them with the lemon juice, the mincemeat and the marzipan.

Melt the butter and add a pinch of cinnamon.

Remember to keep your filo pastry under a damp tea towel to keep it moist.

Take your first sheet of pastry and brush all over with the cinnamon butter, place another sheet on top and brush all over again.

Place 2 heaped dessertspoons of filling at one end, one inch from the end of the pastry, and one inch from the sides, fold over the end to cover the filling.

Fold in both sides and brush with the cinnamon butter, then continue to roll the pastry until it resembles a small spring roll.

When finished making the strudels, place them on a greased baking sheet and brush them all over with the rest of the butter and bake for 30 minutes (150°C / Gas Mark 2) until brown all over.

Brown Sugar Meringues

*Using brown sugar when making meringues gives
them a real "home-made" appearance - a lovely
golden brown colour but chewy in the middle.
Just as meringues should be!*

INGREDIENTS:
5 Egg Whites
5oz (150g) Demerara Sugar
5oz (150g) Caster Sugar

First of all, always have the egg whites at room temperature and
use a large clean bowl and whisk. *An electric mixer gives the
best results.*
Whisk the whites until stiff and starting to peak when you lift up
the whisk. Then gradually whisk in the sugar.
Either pipe the mixture on to baking trays covered with baking
parchment or use 2 dessertspoons to shape the meringues.
Bake in a cool oven (120°C / Gas Mark 1) for one hour and
fifteen minutes.

*The meringues are ready when you can lift them cleanly
off the baking sheet and sound hollow when tapped on
the bottom.*

Debbie's Butterscotch Sauce

*Debbie was our first chef at The Unicorn and has returned
to us on a part-time basis as she is now a busy young mum.
Her bubbliness and enthusiasm never cease to amaze me
and I've got to hand it to her - this sauce is a winner!*

INGREDIENTS:
4 Tablespoons Golden Syrup
4oz (100g) Butter
4oz (100g) Soft Brown Sugar
5fl oz (150ml) Single Cream

Melt all the ingredients except the cream in a pan, stirring
occasionally over a low heat.
Bring to the boil and simmer for a few minutes and remove from
the heat.
When the sauce has cooled, stir in the cream.
Keep in the fridge until needed.

*This sauce is great with meringues and can be served hot
with ice cream.*

Special Thanks to :

Our Parents
Our Customers
Our Staff
Gillian Davidson
John Lamond
Neville Moyer
Brian Ainslie
Debbie Ross
Diane Whitehead
Gladys & Ian Mason ·
Craig Waddell
Scottish Television
CSV Media
Velcropiece
The Gypsy Kings

and especially our children Abby and Katy
for their patience in putting up with absent parents
during the writing of this book.